ARCTIC FOX VS. SNOWY OWL

BY NATHAN SOMMER

BELLWETHER MEDIA • MINNEAPOLIS, MN

TM

Torque brims with excitement
perfect for thrill-seekers of all kinds.
Discover daring survival skills, explore
uncharted worlds, and marvel at mighty
engines and extreme sports. In *Torque* books,
anything can happen. Are you ready?

This edition first published in 2024 by Bellwether Media, Inc.

No part of this publication may be reproduced in whole or in part without written
permission of the publisher. For information regarding permission, write to
Bellwether Media, Inc., Attention: Permissions Department,
6012 Blue Circle Drive, Minnetonka, MN 55343.

Library of Congress Cataloging-in-Publication Data

LC record for Arctic Fox vs. Snowy Owl available at:
https://lccn.loc.gov/2023000637

Text copyright © 2024 by Bellwether Media, Inc. TORQUE and associated logos are
trademarks and/or registered trademarks of Bellwether Media, Inc.

Editor: Kieran Downs   Designer: Josh Brink

Printed in the United States of America, North Mankato, MN.

TABLE OF CONTENTS

THE COMPETITORS

The Arctic is one of the world's toughest places to live. Arctic foxes are built for the cold. Their white fur helps them sneak up on **prey** in the snow.

But snowy owls sometimes challenge Arctic foxes for food. These white birds silently attack their prey. Which Arctic **predator** is stronger?

ARCTIC FOX PROFILE

LENGTH

UP TO 26.8 INCHES
(68 CENTIMETERS)
WITHOUT TAIL

WEIGHT

UP TO 17 POUNDS
(7.7 KILOGRAMS)

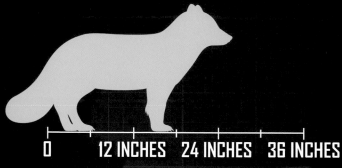

0   12 INCHES   24 INCHES   36 INCHES

HABITAT

 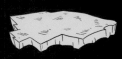

MOUNTAINS   TUNDRA   SEA ICE

ARCTIC FOX RANGE

■ RANGE

Arctic foxes have thick coats, short ears, and long, fluffy tails. Their fur changes colors in different seasons. It is white in the winter. It is gray or brown during warmer months.

These **mammals** are found throughout the Arctic's **tundra**, mountains, and sea ice. They live in dens dug up to 12 feet (3.7 meters) underground.

LONG-LASTING DENS

Some Arctic fox dens have been used for as long as 300 years!

Snowy owls have rounded heads, large bodies, and thick feathers. Males are mostly white. Females have brown spots. These birds of prey have wingspans that stretch up to 4.8 feet (1.5 meters) wide.

Snowy owls live in open areas with few trees. They often sit on hills or near the ground on posts or rocks.

SNOWY OWL PROFILE

WINGSPAN
**UP TO 4.8 FEET
(1.5 METERS)**

WEIGHT
**UP TO 6.5 POUNDS
(2.9 KILOGRAMS)**

0   2 FEET   4 FEET   6 FEET

HABITAT

GRASSLANDS   TUNDRA

SNOWY OWL RANGE

☐ RANGE

SECRET WEAPONS

Arctic foxes have strong senses of smell and hearing. They can smell food up to 24 miles (39 kilometers) away. The foxes can hear **rodents** underneath the snow.

Snowy owls have excellent eyesight. They can spot smaller prey like lemmings from more than 300 feet (91 meters) away. They see larger prey up to 1 mile (1.6 kilometers) away.

A LOT OF LEMMINGS

One snowy owl can eat more than 1,600 lemmings per year.

31 MILES (50 KILOMETERS) PER HOUR

ARCTIC FOX

28 MILES (45 KILOMETERS) PER HOUR

HUMAN

Arctic foxes have furry paw pads. The pads make their footsteps silent on the snow. The pads also help the foxes move on ice. The foxes can run as fast as 31 miles (50 kilometers) per hour in short bursts.

Snowy owls have large wings with special, comb-shaped feathers. They use these to fly without making a sound. Prey do not hear them coming!

SECRET WEAPONS

STRONG SENSES OF SMELL AND HEARING

FURRY PAW PADS

CAMOUFLAGE

Arctic foxes use their fur as **camouflage**. White fur during winter is hard to spot in the snow. Brown fur during warmer months helps them blend into the tundra's plants and rocks.

SNOWY OWL

EXCELLENT EYESIGHT

SILENT FLIGHT

LONG, SHARP TALONS

SNOWY OWL TALON

1.4 INCHES
(3.5 CENTIMETERS)

TALONS

Snowy owls have long, sharp **talons**. These allow the owls to capture prey mid-flight. The powerful talons are also used as weapons to **slash** enemies.

ATTACK MOVES

Arctic foxes become completely still once they hear prey. They tilt their heads to find exactly where it is. Then, they pounce!

Snowy owls quietly watch for prey. Once they spot prey, they silently fly toward it. The owls fly low to the ground. Then, they grab their prey and fly away with it.

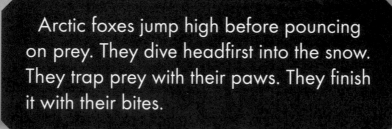

Arctic foxes jump high before pouncing on prey. They dive headfirst into the snow. They trap prey with their paws. They finish it with their bites.

POLAR BEAR FOLLOWERS

Arctic foxes are known to follow polar bears. The foxes eat the remains of what the polar bears kill.

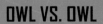

OWL VS. OWL

Snowy owls are known to fight other snowy owls that come near their homes.

Snowy owls fight to protect their nests. They sneak up on and attack enemies who get too close. The birds will even take on wolves!

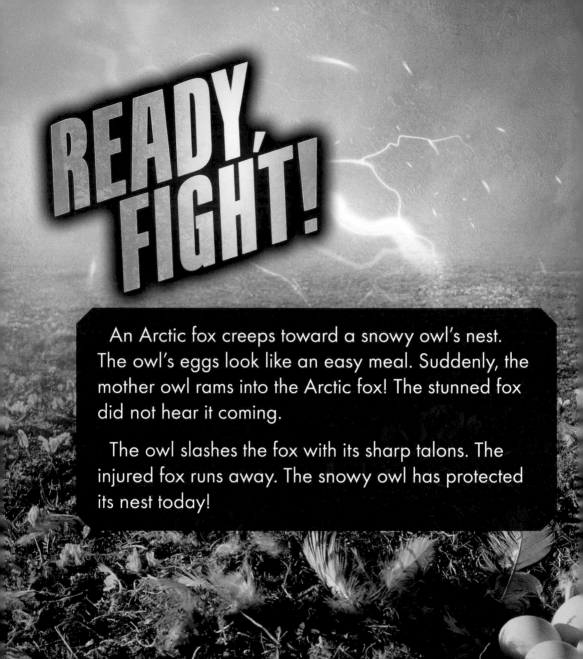

READY, FIGHT!

An Arctic fox creeps toward a snowy owl's nest. The owl's eggs look like an easy meal. Suddenly, the mother owl rams into the Arctic fox! The stunned fox did not hear it coming.

The owl slashes the fox with its sharp talons. The injured fox runs away. The snowy owl has protected its nest today!

GLOSSARY

camouflage—colors and patterns used to help an animal hide in its surroundings

mammals—warm-blooded animals that have backbones and feed their young milk

predator—an animal that hunts other animals for food

prey—animals that are hunted by other animals for food

rodents—small animals that gnaw on their food; mice, rats, and squirrels are all rodents.

slash—to cut with a sharp object

talons—sharp claws on some birds that allow them to grab and tear into prey

tundra—a flat, treeless area where the ground is always frozen

TO LEARN MORE

AT THE LIBRARY

Alkire, Jessie. *Arctic Foxes*. Minneapolis, Minn.: Abdo Publishing, 2019.

Sommer, Nathan. *Golden Eagle vs. Great Horned Owl*. Minneapolis, Minn.: Bellwether Media, 2021.

Wilson, Mark. *The Snowy Owl Scientist*. Boston, Mass.: HarperCollins Publishers, 2022.

ON THE WEB

FACTSURFER

Factsurfer.com gives you a safe, fun way to find more information.

1. Go to www.factsurfer.com

2. Enter "Arctic fox vs. snowy owl" into the search box and click 🔍.

3. Select your book cover to see a list of related content.

INDEX